Your Easy Italian Phrasebook

700 Realistic Italian Phrases for Travel Study and Kids

Your Complete & Practical Italian Phrase Book for Traveling to Italy

2024 Edition

First published 2017 in the United Kingdom

ISBN 978-1-8380606-3-3

© Copyright 2017 by Christian Stahl - All rights reserved

License Notice

This document is geared towards providing exact and reliable information in regard to the topic and issue covered. In no way is it legal to reproduce, duplicate, or transmit any part of this document in either electronic means or in printed format. Recording of this publication is strictly prohibited and any storage of this document is not allowed unless with written permission from the publisher and author.

All rights reserved

The information provided herein is stated to be truthful and consistent, in that any liability, in terms of inattention or otherwise, by any usage or abuse of any policies, processes, or directions contained within is the solitary and utter responsibility of the recipient reader. Under no circumstances will any legal responsibility or blame be held against the publisher for any reparation, damages, or monetary loss due to the information herein, either directly or indirectly. All names and situations are fictional and not related to real persons or events. The information herein is offered for informational purposes solely and is universal as so. The presentation of the information is without contract or any type of guarantee assurance.

Introduction
Pronunciation Guide

Personal Introductions
Everyday Phrases & How to Address Italians
Greetings and Easy Questions
Travel and Hotel Phrases
Restaurants and Eating Out Phrases
Shopping and Renting
Asking Directions
Driving & Parking Phrases
Transportation
Medical Issues and Emergencies
Banking Phrases and Terms
Housekeeping
Christmas
Invitations and Parties
Insurance Phrases and Terms
Real Estate and Terms
Illness and Wellness
Sports Terms and Phrases
University and Education
Computer and Social Media
Small Talk and Getting Things Out of People
Your Workplace
Flights, Airports and Reservations
Taxis and Hiring a Car
Food, Cooking and Diet
Business and Negotiations
Arts and Hobbies
Entertainment and Going Out!
Crime and Help
Rentals and Documents
General Repairs
Church and Religion
Seasons and Holidays
Flirting and Breaking the Ice with Strangers in Italy
Everyday Words for Travelers
Legal Phrases and Terms

Introduction

The book ***Your Easy Italian Phrasebook 700 Realistic Italian Phrases for Travel Study and Kids*** contains proven and realistic phrases for every-day-use, and lessons on the pronunciation of the language.

The first chapters explain the basics of the language and contain proven steps on how to learn Italian in a reasonable short time and to a proper level.

We have prepared over 700 phrases for those with no or very little knowledge and who want to advance their language skills in the shortest time possible.

This book aims to provide a compact resource learning guide that includes essential phrases and terms for most situations.

Pronunciation Guide

Italian spelling is largely phonetic; that is, in most cases a single letter or cluster of letters that represent the same sound, and each sound occurring in the language has only one written representation.

Vowels

There are only 7 Italian vowel sounds, one each for **a**, **i** and **u**; and two vowels each for **e** and **o**.

Italian vowels are *pure*. A sound written with a single letter has a single, unchanged value.

One-sound vowels a, i, u

Italian **a** is long and open. For English speakers, it sounds similar to the short **o** in **shot** or to the first **a** in **mama**. It does not sound like aw or uh

Italian **i** and **u** are relatively easy to pronounce, because they make sounds which usually occur in everyone's English. Italian **i** makes a long **e** sound (for example **steep)**. Italian **u** makes the sound of **oo** like in **boot**.

Two-sound vowels e, o
Each has a so-called "open" and "closed" sound. There is actually only one simple rule for the spoken language: Italian unstressed **e** and **o** are closed sounds

Open **e** has a sound similar to the English short **e**, for example **bet)**; the Italian sound is probably a bit more open (mouth taller). Closed **e** sound more like the **a** in **chaotic**. It's not the same as the English vowel sound in a way, but the slides from the sound goes a little more into **ee**.

Open **o** is like the vowel in **law** or **awe** if you pronounce it without any hint of diphthong. Closed **o**: Most often it's the first vowel sound in **go**, before it turns into **oo**.

Diphthongs

Diphthongs (2 connected vowels) are frequent in Italian.
i is most often pronounced like **y** in **y**ard (for example the word **pietà**)
Otherwise each vowel in a diphthong has its typical sound.

Consonants

Most Italian consonants are similar in pronunciation to English; the consonants *c* and *g* are the only exceptions, because usually they vary according to the letters that follow them.

The **R** Sound
Words you already say in English that have a"rolling **R**".
Butter, cutter, ladder etc
You'll notice what a rolled "R" would sound and feel like the double t's or d's.
You can also try saying "t + d" in a row.

Depending on the region, Italians often drop the final vowel, for example: Pasta e fagioli *pah-stah eh faj-yoh-lee* becoming *pasta fasul fa-zool* and calzone *cal-tso-nay* becoming *cal-zone.*

Double Consonants

Double consonants in Italian should take noticeably longer to pronounce than a corresponding single consonant
For example the double **tt** in **tutto** can and should be make longer

Hard and soft: interactions among c, g, sc, h, and i
As in English, **c** and **g** may be hard or soft. Each consonant is hard when followed by another consonant or by one of the vowels **a**, **o** or **u** and is soft when followed by **e** or **i**. The hard sounds however, are similar to English: **g** as in **good**, **c** as in **car**. Soft **g** is also similar to English, like the **g** in **general**. Italian soft **c** is like English **ch** in **chess**
Another one is the soft sound **sc** is like the sound **sh** makes in **ship**

See the following rules for sounds of consonants

	Sound
c followed by o, a or u like *cosi*	hard c
c followed by consonants other than c like *clemenza*	hard c
c followed by i or e like *città*	soft c

c followed by h like *Pinocchio*	hard c
c followed by i and additional vowel like *pagliaccio*	soft c, silent i

Personal Introductions

1. How are you today?
   Come stai oggi?
   Koh-meh stahy ohj-jee?

2. What's your name? (formal)
   Posso sapere il tuo nome?
   Pos-soh sahpehre eel tuoh no-meh

3. What's your name? (informal, friends)
   Come ti chiami?
   koh-meh tee kyah-mee

9. My name is (first and last name)......
   Il mio nome è (nome e cognome)......
   eel meeoh no-meh eh (no-meh e ko-nyo-meh)

5. I'm pleased to meet you! / Nice to meet you!
   Felice di conoscerti!/ Piacere di conoscerti!
   Feh-ly-ceh diyh koh-noh-skehr-teeh!/ pyah-cheh-reh deeh koh-noh-skehr-teeh!

6. Glad you came
   Sono contento che tu sia venuto
   Soh-noh kohn-teh-ntoh cheh tuh syah veh-nuh-toh

7. It was a pleasure meeting you
   È stato un piacere conoscerti
   Eh stah-toh oohn pyah-cheh-reh koh-noh-skehr-teeh

8. This is my friend John
Lui è Il mio amico John
Loohy eh eel meeh-oh ah-meeh-coh John

9. John, this is my sister Helga
John, lei è mia sorella Helga
jeeohn, leheeh eh myah soh-rehl-lah Hehlgah

Everyday Phrases & How to Address Italians

10. Thank you very much!
Grazie mille!
grah-tsee-eh meehl-leh!

11. All okay
Tutto bene
Tooth-toh beh-neh

12. No thanks
No grazie
Noh grah-tsee-eh

13. You are welcome
Sei il benvenuto
She-eeh eel behn-veh-noo-toh

14. Excuse me, please
Scusami, per favore
skooh-zah-meeh, pehr fah-*voh*-reh

15. Sorry
Scusa
skooh-zah

I am sorry
Mi dispiace
Meeh dees-pyah-cheh

16. This is very kind
Questo è molto gentile
Kweh-stoh eh mohl-toh gehn-teeh-leh

Greetings and Easy Questions

17. Good morning!
    Buongiorno!
    bwohn-johr-noh

18. Good evening
    Buonasera
    bwoh-nah-seh-rah

19. How are you?
    Come stai?
    koh-meh stahy?

20. Very well, thank you.
    Molto bene, grazie.
    mohl-toh beh-neh grah-tsee-eh

21. See you later
    Ci vediamo più tardi
    Ceeh veh-deeh-ah-moh peeh-ooh tahr-deeh

22. Until then
    Fino ad allora
    Feeh-noh ahd ah-hl-oh-rah

23. Good night
    Buonanotte
    bwoh-nah-noht-teh

24. What's going on?
Cosa sta succedendo?
koh-sah stah sooh-hceh-dehn-doh?

25. What's happening?
Che succede?
Cheh soohc-ceh-deh?

26. Let me introduce you to my mother
Lascia che ti presenti mia madre
Lahs-ceeh-ah cheh teeh preh-sehn-teeh meeh-ah mahd-reh

27. Do you have siblings?
Hai fratelli?
Hah-eeh frah-tehl-hleeh?

28. This is my brother
Lui è mio fratello
Looh-eeh eh meeh-oh frah-tehl-loh

29. This is my sister
Lei è mia sorella
Leh-eeh eh meeh-ah soh-rehl-lah

30. This is my uncle
Lui è mio zio
Looh-eeh eh meeh-oh zeeh-oh

31. This is my aunt
Lei è mia zia
leh-eeh eh meeh-ah zeeh-ah

32. This is my grandmother
Lei è mia nonna
leh-eeh eh meeh-ah nohn-nah

33. This is my grandfather
Lui è mio nonno
Looh-eeh eh meeh-oh nohn-noh

34. I have a son / I have a daughter
Ho un figlio/Ho una figlia
Oh oohn feeh-gleeh-oh/ oh oohn-ah feeh-gleeh-ah

35. I am waiting for my mother
Stò aspettando mia madre
Stoh ah-speht-tahn-doh meeh-ah mah-dreh

36. When can we meet?
Quando possiamo incontrarci?
kwahn-doh pohs-seeh-ah-moh een-cohn-trahr-ceeh?

37. Where can we meet?
Dove possiamo incontrarci?
Doh-veh pohs-seeh-ah-moh eehn-cohn-trahr-ceeh?

38. This person is part of my family
Questa persona è parte della mia famiglia
Kwoo-ehs-tah pehr-soh-nah eh pahr-teh dehl-lah meeh-ah fah-meeh-gleeh-ah

39. I have a boyfriend / a girlfriend
Ho un fidanzato/una fidanzata
Oh oohn feeh-dahn-zah-toh/ oohn-ah feehd-ahn-zah-tah

40. I invite you to meet my family
Ti invito a incontrare la mia famiglia
Teeh eehn-vee-toh ah eehn-cohn-trah-reh lah meeh-ah fah-meeh-gleeh-ah

41. Visit me at home
Vieni a tro armi a casa
Veeh-eh-neeh ah troh-vahr-meeh ah cah-sah

42. I want, I don't want
Io voglio, io non voglio
eeh-oh vohg-leeh-oh

43. I would like..
Mi piacerebbe..
Meeh peeh-ah-ceh-rehb-beh

44. Where is..?
Dove è?
Doh-veh eh?

45. How much does it cost?
Quanto costa?
kwahn-toh coh-stah?

46. What time is it?
Che ore sono?
Cheh oh-reh soh-noh?

47. Do you have...?
Hai..?
Ah-eeh...?

48. I have / I don't have...
Io ho/ Io non ho…
Eeh-oh oh/ eeh-oh nohn oh…

49. I understand / I don't understand
Ho capito/ Non ho capito
Oh cah-peeh-toh/ nohn oh cah-peeh-toh

50. Do you understand?
Hai capito?
Ah-eeh cah-peeh-toh?

Travel and Hotel Phrases

51. I am looking for a hotel
Sto cercando un hotel
Stoh cehr-cahn-doh oohn oh-tehl

52. I need a room with a bathroom
Mi serve una stanza con un bagno
Meeh sehr-veh oohn-ah stahn-zah cohn oohn bah-gnoh

53. Do you have a cheaper room?
Avete una stanza più economica?
Ah-veh-teh ooh-nah stahn-zah peeh-ooh eh-coh-noh-meeh-cah?

54. Can you call me a taxi, please?
Per favore, può chiamarmi un taxi?
Pehr fah-voh-reh, pooh-oh cheeh-ah-mahr-meeh oohn tah-xeeh?

55. Bring me to the airport!
Mi porti all'aereoporto!
Meeh pohr-teeh ahll-ah-eh-reh-oh-pohr-toh!

56. When is the next flight to..?
A che ora c'è il prossimo volo per...?
Ah cheh oh-rah ceh eel prohs-seeh-moh voh-loh pehr

57. At what time does the flight from...arrive?
Quando arriverà il volo da..?
kwahn-doh ahr-reeh-veh-rah eel voh-loh dah..?

58. Where is the exchange?
Dove c'è lo scambio?
Doh-veh ceh loh scahm-beeh-oh?

59. Where is the bank?
Dove è la banca?
Doh-veh eh lah bahn-cah?

60. Where is the bus station?
Dov'è la stazione dei bus?
Doh-veh lah stah-zeeh-oh-neh deh-eeh boohs?

61. Where can I buy a ticket to...?
Dove posso comprare un biglietto per…?
Doh-veh pohs-soh cohm-prah-reh oohn beeh-gleeh-eht-toh pehr…?

62. I pay the ticket with my credit card
Pago il biglietto con la mia carta di credito
Pah-goh eel beeh-gleeh-eht-toh cohn lah meeh-ah cahr-tah deeh creh-deeh-toh

Restaurants and Eating Out Phrases

63. I like to order a coffee
Vorrei ordinare un caffè
vohr-reh-eeh ohr-dee-nah-reh oohn cahf-feh

64. Can I have the menu please?
Posso avere il menu, per favore?
Pohs-soh ah-veh-reh eel meh-nooh, pehr fah-voh-reh?

65. We would like to reserve a table
Vorremmo prenotare un tavolo
Vohr-rehm-moh preh-noh-tah-reg oohn tah-voh-loh

66. Do you have vegetarian meals?
Avete piatti vegetariani?
Ah-veh-teh peeh-aht-teeh veh-geh-tah-reeh-ah-neeh?

67. I like to have my steak medium rare –
Vorrei avere la mia bistecca con cottura media
Vohr-reh-eeh ah-veh-reh lah meeh-ah beehs-tehc-cah cohn coht-tooh-rah meh-deeh-ah

68. The food is unacceptable
Il cibo è inacettabile
Eel ceeh-boh eh eeh-nah-ceht-tah-beeh-leh

69. Bring me something else
Portami qualcos'altro
Pohr-tah-meeh qooh-ahl-coh-sahl-troh

70. I would like to order a glass of white wine
Vorrei ordinare un bicchiere di vino bianco
Vohr-reh-eeh ohr-deeh-nah-reh oohn beehc-cheeh-eh-reh deeh vih-noh beeh-ahn-coh

71. The bill / check please –
Il conto/fattura per favore
Eel cohn-toh/faht-tooh-rah pehr fah-voh-reh

72. The tip is not included
La mancia non è inclusa
Lah mahn-ceeh-ah nohn eh eehn-clooh-sah

Shopping and Renting

73. We are looking for a good souvenir
Stiamo cercando un bel souvenir
Steeh-ah-moh cehr-cahn-doh oohn behl sooh-veh-neehr

74. Do you have a larger size?
This is too small
Avete una taglia più larga?
Questa è troppo piccola
Ah-veh-teh oohn-ah tah-gleeh-ah peeh-ooh lahr-gah?
Kwooh-ehs-tah eh trohp-poh peehc-coh-lah

75. Esta camiseta es demasiada cara
Questa maglia è troppo costosa
Kwooh-ehs-tah mah-gleeh-ah eh trohp-poh cohs-toh-sah

76. Is the price negotiable?
Il prezzo è trattabile?
Eel prehz-zoh eh traht-tah-beeh-leh?

77. I only want to buy fresh ingredients
Voglio comprare solo ingredienti freschi
Voh-gleeh-oh cohm-prah-reh soh-loh eehn-greh-deeh-ehn-teeh frehs-cheeh

78. How much is the weekly rent?
Quanto costa l'affitto settimanale?
Kwooh-ahn-toh cohs-tah lahf-feeht-toh seht-teeh-mah-nah-leh?

79. Do we have to pay a deposit?
Dobbiamo pagare un deposito?
Dohb-beeh-ah-moh pah-gah-reh oohn deh-poh-seeh-toh?

80. We are looking for a furnished room
Stiamo cercando una stanza arredata
Steeh-ah-moh cehr-cahn-doh oohn-ah stahn-zah ahr-reh-dah-tah

81. We like to rent this room by the month
Vorremmo affittare questa stanza per tutto il mese
Vohr-rehm-moh ahf-feeht-tah-reh kwooh-ehs-tah stahn-zah pehr tooht-toh eel meh-seh

82. When do I get my money back?
Quando riavrò I miei soldi?
Kwooh-ahm-doh reeh-ahv-roh eeh meeh-eh-eeh sohl-deeh?

83. The house needs to be cleaned
La casa ha bisogno di essere pulita
Lah cah-sah ah beeh-soh-gnoh deeh ehs-seh-reh pooh-leeh-tah

Asking Directions

84. Where is..?
Dove è…?
Doh-veh eh…?

85. Can you tell me the way to..?
Puoi dirmi la strada per…?
Pooh-oh-eeh deehr-meh lah strah-dah pehr…?

86. Can you show me on the map?
Puoi farmelo vedere sulla mappa?
Pooh-oh-eeh fahr-meh-loh veh-deh-reh soohl-la mahp-pah?

87. Can you walk?
Puoi camminare?
Pooh-oh-eeh cahm-meeh-nah-reh?

88. Where are the toilets?
Dove sono I bagni?
Doh-veh soh-noh ee bah-gneeh

89. Is it near?
È vicino?
Eh veeh-ceeh-noh

90. Is it far?
È lontano?
Eh lohn-tah-noh?

91. Is there a bus?
C'è un bus?
Ceh oohn boohs?

92. Where does this road go to?
Dove porta questa strada?
Doh-veh pohr-tah kwooh-ehs-tah strah-dah?

93. Which direction?
Quale direzione?
Kwooh-ah-leh deeh-reh-zeeh-oh-neh?

94. I am looking for the next exit
Stò cercando la prossima uscita
Stoh cehr-cahn-doh lah prohs-seeh-mah oohs-ceeh-tah

95. Is this the street to...?
È questa la strada per...?
Eh kwooh-ehs-tah lah strah-dah pehr...?

96. Where can I find the....?
Dove posso trovare il..?
Doh-veh pohs-soh troh-vah-reh eel...?

97. Left
Sinistra
Seeh-neehs-trah

98. Right
Destra
Dehs-trah

99. Turn right
Gira a destra
Geeh-rah ah dehs-trah

100. On the corner
All'angolo
Ahl-lahn-goh-loh

101. Opposite the gas / petrol station
Di fronte al distributore di benzina
Deeh frohn-teh ahl deehs-treeh-booh-toh-reh deeh behn-zeeh-nah

102. You have to go back
Devi tornare indietro
Deh-veeh tohr-nah-reh eehn-deeh-eh-troh

103. Keep going straight ahead
Continua ad andare avanti
Cohn-teehn-ooh-ah ahd ahn-dah-reh ah-vahn-teeh

104. Take the road for...
Prendi la strada per...
Prehn-deeh lah strah-dah pehr

105. Under the bridge
Sotto il ponte
Soht-toh eel pohn-teh

106. At the crossroads
All'incrocio
Ahl-leehn-croh-ceeh-oh

107. You go as far as..
Sei andato così lontano
Seh-eeh ahn-dah-toh coh-seeh lohn-tah-noh

108. ….next to the supermarket
….vicino al supermercato
…veeh-ceeh-noh ahl sooh-pehr-mehr-cah-toh

109. To cross the street
Attraversa la strada
Aht-trah-vehr-sah lah strah-dah

110. On the second floor
Al secondo piano
Ahl she-cohn-doh peeh-ah-noh

111. The supermarket is in front of the church.
Il supermercato è davanti alla chiesa
Eel *sooh-pehr-mehr-cah-toh eh dah-vahn-teeh ahl-lah cheeh-eh-sah*

112. The embassy is across the street.
L'ambasciata è dall'altra parte della strada
Lahm-bahs-ceeh-ah-tah eh dahl-lahl-trah pahr-teh dehl-lah strah-dah

113. The hospital is around the corner
L'ospedale è dietro l'angolo
Lohs-peh-dah-leh eh deeh-eht-roh lahn-goh-loh

114. How long will it take?
Quanto tempo ci vorrà?
Kwooh-ahn-toh tehm-poh ceeh vohr-rah?

115. You go straight, and then you turn left.
Devi andare Avanti e poi girare a sinistra
Deh-veeh ahn-dah-reh ah-vahn-teeh eh poh-eeh geeh-rah-reh ah seeh-neehs-trah

Driving & Parking Phrases

116. Is the traffic heavy?
Il traffico è intenso?

117. Is there a different way to the airport?
C'è un altra strada per l'aereoporto?

118. What is causing this traffic jam?
Cosa causa l'ingorgo?

119. When will the road be clear?
Quando sarà ripulita la strada?

120. What is the speed limit?
Quale è il limite di velocità

121. Is there a toll on this motorway?
C'è un pedaggio in que sta autostrada?

122. Can you clean the windscreen?
Puoi pulire il parabrezza?

123. We got lost!
Ci siamo persi!

124. Slow the car down
Ferma la macchina

125. Can you drive faster?
Puoi guidare più veloce?

126. I need to get out here
Devo uscire di qui

127. We are looking for a gas / petrol station
Stiamo cercando un distributore di benzina

128. Can I park here?
Posso parcheggiare qui?

129. Where is the nearest parking garage?
Dove è il parcheggio più vicino?

130. How long can I stay here?
Per quanto posso stare qui?

131. Where do I pay?
Dove devo pagare?

132. Fill the tank please
Riempi la tanica, per favore

133. This is my drivers license
Questa è la mia patente

Transportation

134. Where is the airport?
Dove è l'aereoporto?

135. Where is the train station?
Dove è la stazione?

136. Where is the ticket machine?
Dove è la macchina dei biglietti?

137. Is that within walking distance?
È senza distanza di sicurezza?

138. Where do I transfer?
Dove mi devo trasferire?

139. How much luggage may I bring?
Quanti bagagli posso portare?

140. At what gate will I find the airplane?
A quale gate troverò l'aereoplano?

141. The flight has been delayed
Il volo è stato ritardato

142. Does this bus stop in Granada too? –
Questo bus si ferma anche a Granada?

143. Is there a stopover?
    C'è una sosta?

144. Is there public transportation?
    Ci sono trasporti pubblici?

145. When do we arrive?
    Quando arriveremo?

146. What is the name of the next station?
    Quale è il nome della prossima stazione?

147. Where do we go?
    Dove andiamo?

Medical Issues and Emergencies

148. Where is the next hospital?
Dove è il prossimo ospedale?

149. Our insurance in the US will pay for this
La nostra assicurazione in America pagherà per questo

150. My wife needs surgery
Mia moglie ha bisogno di un operazione

151. I need to have my tooth fixed
Devo sistemare il mio dente

152. Do you have painkillers?
Hai antidolorifici?

153. I am allergic against... (fish) –
Sono allergico al .. (pesce)

154. I had an accident, send an ambulance –
Ho avuto un incidente, manda un ambulanza

155. I need a remedy against headache-
Mi serve un rimedio contro il mal di testa

156. I cut myself, do you have a bandage?
Mi sono tagliato, hai un cerotto?

157. Can you send a doctor to my house?
Puoi mandare un dottore a casa mia?

Banking Phrases and Terms

158. I am looking for an ATM
Sto cercando un bancomat

159. Do they change dollars?
Cambiano I dollari?

160. I'd like to open a checking account
Vorrei aprire un conto

170. I like to open a savings account.
Vorrei aprire un conto corrente

171. What documents do I need?
Di quali documenti ho bisogno?

172. The ATM machine did not dispense notes
Il bancomat non fornisce il promemoria

173. I want to apply for a personal credit
Voglio richiedere un conto personale

174. I want to cash a cheque
Voglio incassare un assegno

175. I need cash money from my account
Mi servono contanti dal mio conto

Housekeeping

176. We need a charlady / maid
Ci serve una domestica/cameriera

177. Please clean the corners too
Per favore pulisci anche gli angoli

178. Clean the carpet with a vacuum cleaner
Pulisci il tappeto con un aspirapolvere

179. Please clean the windows
Per favore pulisci le finestre

180. Put the bottles into the refrigerator
Metti le bottiglie nel frigo

181. You have to make the bed too
Devi anche fare il letto

182. Can you water the plants please?
Puoi annaffiare le piante, per favore?

183. Turn down the heating
Abbassa il riscaldamento

184. Screw a new light bulb into the lamp
Avvita una nuova lampadina nel lampadario

185. to mop the floor
Pulisci il pavimento

186. Bring the trash outside
Porta fuori la spazzatura

187. Please empty the buckets
Per favore svuota I secchi

188. Carry the cases into the basement
Porta le scatole in cantina

189. Clean the closets too
Pulisci anche gli armadi

190. Fluff and shake the pillows
Piega e scuoti I cuscini

191. Close the shutters
Chiudi le persiane

192. Don't forget to lock the doors
Non dimenticarti di chiudere le porte

193. To paint the wall
Dipingere il muro

194. Roll up the carpets!
Arrotolare I tappeti!

195. The bathroom needs to be cleaned
Il bagno ha bisogno di essere pulito

196. Polish the mirrors!
Lucida gli specchi!

197. You are not allowed to make a break / no pause
Non hai il permesso di fare un break/ nessuna pausa

198. We pay once a month
Paghiamo una volta al mese

199. Open all the windows!
Apri tutte le finestre!

200. We appreciate your good work
Apprezziamo il tuo buon lavoro

201. Housekeeping
Faccende domestiche

Christmas
Natale

201. We are looking for a Christmas gift
Stiamo cercando un regalo di Natale

202. Where are the Christmas markets?
Dove sono I mercatini di Natale?

203. Can you wrap it up please?
Può fare un pacchetto per favore?

204. Do they have a Santa Claus in ......?
Hanno Babbo Natale a ..?

205. We love Christmas time
Noi amiamo il Natale

206. Christmas songs are important
Le canzone di Natale sono importanti

207. We are looking for a Christmas tree
Stiamo cercando un albero di Natale

208. We need help to decorate it
Ci serve aiuto per decorarlo

209. We are going to visit our family for Christmas
Noi andremo a visitare la nostra famiglia per Natale

210. What do you have for Christmas dinner?
Cosa avrai per il pranzo di Natale?

211. We only go to church at Christmas
Andiamo in chiesa solo a Natale

212. I have a Christmas gift for you
Ho un regalo di Natale per te

Invitations and Parties

213. Please lay the table for dinner
Per favore, prepara il tavolo per la cena

214. You are invited
Sei invitato

215. Welcome you to our house
Benvenuto nella nostra casa

216. Please come in
Per favore entra

217. We have prepared dinner for you
Abbiamo preparato la cena per te

218. You can bring your family
Puoi portare la tua famiglia

219. Tonight we are expecting guests
Questa sera aspettiamo ospiti

220. I have received an invitation
Io ho ricevuto un invito

221. We are all one family
Siamo tutti una famiglia

222. This is the key for the main entrance
Questa è la chiave dell'ingresso principale

223. This is the key for the room
Questa è la chiave della stanza

224. Where can we leave our luggage?
Dove possiamo lasciare I nostri bagagli?

225. I would like to invite you
Mi piacerebbe invitarti

226. We want to cancel our reservation
Vogliamo cancellare la nostra prenotazione

227. We are organizing a barbecue evening
Stiamo organizzando una serata barbecue

228. We have a bathroom for men and for women
Abbiamo un bagno per uomini e per le donne

229. Do you have a guest house ?
Hai una casa per gli ospiti?

230. We prefer to sleep in a private room
Noi preferiamo dormire in una stanza privata

231. We had a great time
Noi ci siamo divertiti

232. There is no smoking in the room
Non c'è fumo nella stanza

234. Can you please turn down the volume?
Per favore puoi abbassare il volume?

235. Please take the trash outside
Per favore porta fuori la spazzatura

236. Please clean the room before you leave
Per favore, pulisci la stanza prima di partire

237. There is a cleaning fee.
Ecco la tassa di pulizia

238. You have damaged something
Hai danneggiato qualcosa

Insurance Phrases and Terms

239. Do you have insurance?
Hai un assicurazione?

240. Is your car insured
La tua macchina è assicurata?

241. Do you have accident insurance?
Hai un assicurazione sugli incidenti?

242. We would like to insure the car
Noi vorremmo assicurare la macchina

243. I need a household insurance
Mi serve un assicurazione domestica

244. Let me get my insurance papers
Fammi prendere I miei documenti di assicurazione

245. I have everything insured
Io ho assicurato tutto

246. We should file the police report
Dovremmo presentare il resoconto della polizia

247. We should file a damage report
Dovremmo presentare un resoconto dei danni

248. Are they going to raise our premiums?
Loro ci alzeranno I nostri premi?

249. We don't agree with appraisal
Noi non siamo d'accordo con la perizia

250. I am the beneficiary
Io sono il beneficiario

251. We need a free tariff
Noi abbiamo bisogno di un tariffario

252. Where can I buy a car insurance
Dove posso comprare un assicurazione auto

253. I need a health insurance
Ho bisogno di un assicurazione sanitaria

254. We'd like to insure our property
Noi vorremmo assicurare la nostra proprietà

255. Can we pay by annual installments?
Possiamo pagare una rata annuale?

256. How much are the deductibles?
Quanto possiamo dedurre?

257. I need a travel insurance.
Mi serve un assicurazione sui viaggi

258. Signing of a contract
Firma di un contratto

259. I need a life insurance
Ho bisogno di un assicurazione sulla vita

Real Estate and Terms

260. What kind of neighbors do we have here?
Che tipo di vicinato abbiamo qui?

261. When was this house built?
Quando è stata costruita questa casa?

262. How much is the property / land tax?
A quanto ammonta la tassa di proprietà?

263. How much are the running costs?
A quanto ammontano I costi di gestione?

264. We would like to view the house
Noi vorremmo vedere la casa

265. Are you the owner of this property?
Sei il proprietario di questa proprietà?

266. Is this house rented?
Questa casa è affittata?

267. Who is living in this house?
Chi vive in questa casa?

268. Is there a community pool?
C'è una piscine comunale?

269. How much is the administration fee?
A quanto ammonta la quota amministrativa?

270. How many square meters has the land?
Quanti metri quadri ha la proprietà?

271. How many floors has this house?
Quanti piani ha questa casa?

272. This house needs to be renovated
Questa casa ha bisogno di essere rinnovata

273. How many people are registered in the deed?
Quante persone sono registrate negli atti?

274. Do you have a floor plan?
Hai una pianta del piano?

275. Is this house owned by the bank?
Questa casa è di proprietà della banca?

276. We don't need a realtor
Non ci serve un agente immobiliare

277. Is the house rented?
La casa è affittata?

278. Do you offer financing?
Offrite un finanziamento?

Illness and Wellness

279. I am sick
Sono malato

280. I don't feel well
Non mi sento bene

281. I need a doctor who speaks English
Mi serve un dottore che parli inglese

282. I need a dentist
Mi serve un dentista

283. It's an emergency
È un emergenza

284. I need an appointment
Mi serve un appuntamento

285. My back hurts
La mia schiena fa male

286. I need medicine
Ho bisogno delle medicine

287. My throat bothers me
La mia gola di fa male

288. I have pain in my chest
Ho un dolore al petto

289. My stomach hurts
Ho mal di stomaco

290. My foot is inflamed
Ho il piede infiammato

291. I broke my arm
Mi sono rotto il braccio

292. I prefer natural product
Preferisco I prodotti naturali

293. I am infected with S.T.D.
Sono infetto da una malattia venerea

294. I have diabetes
Ho il diabete

296. I have liver problems
Ho problemi al fegato

297. Is my disease serious?
Il mio diabete è grave?

298. I have a terminal illness
Ho una malattia terminale

299. It hurts in this part
Fa male da questa parte

300. I need painkillers
Ho bisogno di antidolorifici

301. I need a check-up
Ho bisogno di un check-up

302. I need new glasses
Ho bisogno di nuovi occhiali

303. I need a prescription for..
Ho bisogno di una ricrtta per..

304. Where can I find a specialist for..?
Dove posso trovare uno specialita per..?

305. I have private insurance
Ho un assicurazione privata

306. I need pills against..
Ho bisogno di pillole contro..

307. I need a diagnostic
Ho bisogno di una diagnosi

308. Can you call a doctor?
Puoi chiamare un dottore?

309. Can you call an ambulance?
Puoi chiamare un ambulanza?

310. Can you drive me to the hospital?
Puoi portarmi all'ospedale?

311. I am suffering under pain
Stò soffrendo sotto pena

312. I suffer from indigestion
Stò soffrendo di indigestione

313. I have to threw up
Io ho vomitato

314. I am dizzy
Ho le vertigini

315. I cut myself
Mi sono tagliato

316. I need band aid
Mi serve un bendaggio

317. Where is the next pharmacy?
Dove è la prossima farmacia?

318. Does the medicine cause side effects?
La medicina può causare effetti collaterali?

Sports Terms and Phrases

319. We like soccer
Ci piace il calcio

320. When does the game start?
Quando inizia la partita?

321. Are you a fan of...?
Sei un fan di..?

322. Can we join the group?
Possiamo unirci al gruppo?

323. We like sports
Ci piacciono gli sport

324. We play a game
Noi giochiamo a un gioco

325. Where can we rent a bicycle?
Dove possiamo noleggiare una bicicletta?

326. Is there a gym here?
C'è una palestra qui?

327. How much is membership?
Quanto costa l'iscrizione?

328. I need to make exercise to lose weight
Ho bisogno di fare esercizi per perdere peso

329. I like to play tennis
Mi piace giocare a tennis

330. I like to swim
Mi piace nuotare

331. I am looking for a yoga group
Sto cercando un gruppo Yoga

332. I try to find a fitness instructor
Sto cercando di trovare un istruttore di fitness

333. Can you help me to lift the weights?
Puoi aiutarmi a sollevare I pesi?

334. I need aerobics
Ho bisogno di aerobica

335. I have to start slowly
Io devo iniziare lentamente

336. We are looking for a good diving spot
Noi stiamo cercando un buon punto per lanciarci

University and Education

337. Where can I register?
Dove posso registrarmi?

338. When is semester break?
Quando c'è la pausa del semestre?

339. What is your principle area of study?
Quale è la tua principale area di studi?

340. When is the examen
Quando c'è l'esame?

341. Let's to to the university!
Facciamo l'università!

342. What is the campus policy?
Cosa è la politica del campus?

343. How much is the tuition fee?
A quanto ammonta la tassa di iscrizione?

344. Are there still enrollment places available?
Ci sono ancora posti disponibili?

345. What are the degree courses?
Cosa sono I corsi di laurea?

346. Do they offer financial aid?
Loro offrono supporto finanziario?

347. What major degrees do they offer ?
Quali lauree offrono?

348. Where can I study ….best?
Dove posso studiare.. meglio?

349. Is the food in the canteen edible?
Il cibo della mensa è commestibile?

350. Where can I get the learning material?
Dove posso predere il materiale didattico?

351. I meet you in the auditorium
Ti incontro nell'auditorium

352. This university has a entrance examination
L'università ha un test di ingresso

Computer and Social Media

353. Can I join your group?
Posso unirmi al vostro gruppo?

354. Is advertising allowed?
La pubblicità è permessa?

355. I would like to participate
Io vorrei partecipare

356. What are the rules for this group?
Quali sono le regole di questo gruppo?

357. Spam is prohibited
Lo spam è proibito

358. Can you help me to find ....?
Puoi aiutarmi a trovare...?

359. Can you help me to install a program?
Puoi aiutarmi ad installare un programma?

360. I need original components
Io ho bisogno di componenti originali

361. Does it come with a cable?
Arriva con un cavo?

362. The printer doesn't print
La stampante non stampa

363. Where can I buy printer cartridges?
Dove posso comprare cartucce per stampante?

364. Where to they repair computer nearby?
Dove riparano computer nelle vicinanze?

365. My tablet needs a new glass
Il mio tablet ha bisogno di un nuovo vetro

366. Where can I download this?
Dove lo posso scaricare?

Small Talk and Getting Things Out of People

367. What is your profession?
Che lavoro fai?

368. I work for the ... company
Io lavoro per la compagnia..

369 I have my own business
Io ho il mio business

370. I am employed
Sono un impiegato

371. I am a student
Sono uno studente

372. I have an online business
Ho un business online

373. I live alone
Io vivo solo

374. I have two children
Ho due bambini

375 I am married
Io sono sposato

376. Where do you live
Dove vivi

377. Do you have an address?
Hai un indirizzo?

378. I live in Rome
Io vivo a Roma

378. Do you live in .....?
Vivi a ..?

378. Tomorrow we have a party
Domani noi abbiamo una festa

378. My uncle is visiting me
Mio zio mi stà visitando

379. Do you have siblings
Hai fratelli

380. Shall I bring something?
Io devo portare qualcosa?

381 May I bring my dog?
Posso portare il mio cane?

382. We have a house in the center
Noi abbiamo una casa in centro

Your Workplace

383. He / she is calling
Lui/lei sta chiamando

384. I'd like to speak with Mr./Ms. ….
Io vorrei parlare con il Signor/la Signora…

385. The line is busy
La linea è occupata

386. What time suits you?
A che ora vi va bene?

387. Can I have a receipt please?
Posso avere una ricevuta per favore?

388. My boss said …
Il mio capo ha detto..

389. I need a hard copy
Io ho bisogno di una copia cartacea

390. Did you get my mail?
Avevi ricevuto la mia mail?

391. I'd like to make an appointment
Io vorrei prendere un appuntamento

392. Can we meet on Thursday morning?
Possiamo incontrarci Giovedì mattina?

393. This is part of my job
Questo è parte del mio lavoro

393. Where can I get internet around here?
Dove posso accedere a Internet qui intorno?

394. I have already finished my work
Io ho già finito il mio lavoro

394. Have a nice trip / a good vacation
Buon viaggio/ buona vacanza

Flights, Airports and Reservations

396. What is our flight number?
Quale è il numero del nostro volo?

397. I have a reservation
Ho una prenotazione

398. have only one suitcase
Ho solo una valigia

399. I have only hand luggage
Ho solo un bagaglio a mano

400. Can we take that into the cabin?
Possiamo portarlo dentro la cabina?

401. Do I need a visa?
Ho bisogno di una visa?

402. Where do I claim the luggage?
Dove posso reclamare il bagaglio?

403. Where can we find the gate number.. ?
Dove possiamo trovare il gate numero..?

404. I need to change my ticket
Ho bisogno di cambiare il mio biglietto

405. The airline changed our flight
La compagnia aerea ha cambiato il nostro volo

406. I would like to have a window seat
Io vorrei avere un posto al finestrino

407. I would like to have an aisle seat
Io vorrei avere un posto sul corridoio

408. Can I get an upgrade?
Posso avere un aggiornamento?

409. Do we have to go through security?
Dobbiamo andare attraverso la sicurezza?

410. Where is the information desk?
Dove è il banco informazioni?

411. This computer belongs to me
Questo computer appartiene a me

412. I have nothing to declare
Non ho niente da dichiarar

412. Do you know at what time are we arriving?
Sai a che ora arriveremo?

413. I would like to change my seat
Vorrei cambiare il mio posto

414. Where does this plane fly to?
Dove è diretto questo volo?

415. Where is the arrival terminal?
Dove è il terminal degli arrivi?

415. Where is the terminal for departure?
Dove è il terminal delle partenze?

416. Our suitcase has been stolen!
La nostra valigia è stata rubata!

417. Do you have a hotel voucher?
Hai un voucher per l'hotel?

418. Where do I find the shuttle transfer to Terminal1?
Dove posso trovare la navetta per il Terminal 1?

419. Where do I find the car rental companies?
Dove posso trovare le compagnie di noleggio auto?

Taxis and Hiring a Car

420. We would like to rent a car
Noi vorremmo noleggiare una macchina

421. We had an accident
Abbiamo avuto un incidente

422. They have towed the car!
Loro hanno trainato l'auto!

423. I need a tow truck
Ho bisogno di un carro attrezzi

424. The car has a flat tire
L'auto ha una gomma bucata

425. The car won't start
L'auto non vuole partire

426. The car has a scratch
L'auto ha un graffio

427. Can you recommend a garage?
Puoi raccomandare un garage?

428. Can you repair the car?
Puoi riparare l'auto?

429. How long does it take?
Quanto tempo ci vorrà?

430. Where can I return the car?
Dove posso restituire l'auto?

Food, Cooking and Diet

431. What is your favorite food?
Quale è il tuo cibo preferito?

432. Can you please say what this is?
Puoi dirmi per favore cosa è questo?

433. It tastes very interesting
Ha un sapore interessante

434. This is very delicious / This is disgusting
Questo è delizioso / Questo è disgustoso

435. Bring everything at once
Porta tutto in una volta

436. Can you bring us a larger portion please?
Puoi portarci una porzione più grande per favore?

437. What are the ingredients for this dish?
Quali sono gli ingredienti per questo piatto?

438. How do you make paella?
Come cucini la paella?

439. We eat traditional food
Noi mangiamo cibo tradizionale

440. We are on a diet
Noi siamo a dieta

441. How many calories are in there?
Quante calorie ci sono qua dentro?

442. What dish do you recommend?
Che piatto ci consigli?

443. What international dishes do you offer
Che piatti internazionali offri?

444. What are typical local ingredients?
Quali sono gli ingredienti tipici locali?

445. First fry it then you bake it
Prima friggilo poi infornalo

446. We prefer a strong flavor
Noi preferiamo un gusto forte

447. We cook at home
Noi cuciniamo a casa

448. How do you cook this dish?
Come cucini questo piatto?

449. We are looking for a supermarket
Noi stiamo cercando un supermercato

Business and Negotiations

450. I need a receipt / bill
Io ho bisogno di una ricetta/ fattura

451. This is a bad ripp-off
Questa è una fregatura

452. Thank's, but I am not interested
Grazie, ma non sono interessato

453. I want to speak with the owner!
Voglio parlare con il titolare!

454. I the price negotiable?
Il prezzo è trattabile?

455. This is my team
Questa è la mia squadra

456. We should make a contract
Noi dovremmo sottoscrivere un contratto

457. We pay later
Noi pagheremo piu tardi

458. We order tomorrow
Noi ordineremo domani

459. When can you deliver?
Quando potete spedire?

460. Who is paying customs?
Chi sta pagando la dogana?

461. How much are the total costs?
A quanto ammonta il totale?

462. What is your best price?
Quale è il tuo prezzo migliore?

463. We want to cancel
Noi vogliamo cancellare

464. It is too expensive
Costa troppo

465. Are taxes included?
Le tasse sono incluse?

466. How much is the commission?
A quanto ammonta la commissione?

467. I need to write it down
Io ho bisogno di scriverlo

468. I need this in writing
Mi serve un testo scritto

469. What are the delivery terms?
Quali sono le modalità di consegna?

470. Does this product has warranties?
Questo prodotto ha la garanzia?

471. We like to place an order
Noi vorremmo ordinare

472. We make you an offer
Vi facciamo un offerta

473. We accept your offer
Accettiamo l'offerta

474. We reject your offer
Rifiutiamo l'offerta

475. We pay after delivery
Noi paghiamo dopo la spedizione

476. We pay now
Noi paghiamo adesso

477. Is there a discount?
C'è uno sconto?

478. Do you accept credit cards?
Accetti carte di credito?

Arts and Hobbies

479. Where is the museum?
Dove è il museo?

480. This is magnificent
Questo è magnifico

481. Who built all of this?
Chi ha costruito tutto questo?

482. What's the name of the artist?
Quale è il nome dell'artista?

483. We appreciate art
Noi apprezziamo l'arte

484. Do you know the artist?
Tu conosci l'artista?

485. How did they clean the sculpture?
Come hanno pulito la scultura?

486. This is a beautiful painting
Questo è un bellissimo dipinto

487. How old is it?
Quanti anni ha?

488. Does it have a signature?
Ha una firma?

489. This is rare
Questo è raro

490. What's the name of this style?
Quale è il nome di questo stile?

491. Are you an expert?
Sei un esperto?

492. We are only interested in authentic arts
Noi siamo interessati solo ad arte autentica

493. This is only of personal value
Questo è solo un valore affettivo

494. Is this original?
Questo è originale?

Is this part of your hobby?
Questo è parte del tuo hobby?

Entertainment and Going Out!

495. Tonight we go out
Stasera usciamo

496. We go to a concert
Noi andiamo a un concerto

497. How much are the tickets?
Quanto costano I biglietti?

498. We will meet at the entrance
Ci incontreremo all'entrata

499. What movie will we watch?
Che film vedremo?

500. Did you like the movie?
Ti è piaciuto il film?

501. Is there a good night club?
C'è un bel night club qui?

502. Do you like dancing?
Ti piace ballare?

503. Can I go with you?
Posso venire con te?

504. This is fun!
Questo è divertente!

505. This is boring.
Questo è noioso.

506. Are you coming with me?
Stai venendo con me?

507. Do they have a botanical garden here?
Hanno un giardino botanico qui?

508. Is there a public swimming pool?
C'è una piscina pubblica qui?

509. Which museum can you recommend?
Quale museo ci consigli?

510. We are looking for a spa
Noi stiamo cercando una spa

520. Where can I get a massage?
Dove posso avere un massaggio?

521. Is the movie in original language?
Il film è in lingua originale?

Crime and Help

522. I need a doctor
Ho bisogno di un dottore

523. I need help!
Ho bisogno di aiuto!

524. Call the police!
Chiama la polizia!

525. I am going to call the police
Sto andando a chiamare la polizia

526. This is an emergency
Questa è un emergenza

527. Stop the thief!
Ferma il ladro!

528. I am the witness
Io sono il testimone

529. I have not seen anything
Io non ho visto nulla

530. I have been robbed
Io sono stato derubato

531. I have been attacked
Io sono stato attaccato

532. The broke into my apartment
Sono entrati nel mio appartamento

533. They stole my wallet
Hanno rubato il mio portafogli

534. I have a complaint
Io ho una denuncia

535. I want to file a police report
Io voglio compilare un resoconto

536. I need to contact my embassy
Io devo contattare la mia ambasciata

527. I want to speak with a lawyer
Voglio parlare con un avvocato

538. I lost my money
Ho perso I miei soldi

539. I forgot my passport
Ho dimenticato il mio passaporto

540. I left the keys in the room
Ho lasciato le chiavi nella stanza

541. I have to leave now!
Devo andare adesso!

Rentals and Documents

542. I want to hire a car
Io voglio noleggiare un auto

543. I need it for one week
Mi serve per una settimana

544. Please explain the documents
Per favore spiegami I documenti

545. Must I return the car here?
Devo restituire l'auto qui?

546. Is there a charge per kilometre?
C'è una tariffa a kilometri?

547. Please show me how to operate the car?
Per favore mi puoi fare vedere come aprire l'auto?

548. I would like to rent a small size car
Io vorrei noleggiare un auto piccola

550. Do you have a car with automatic?
Hai un auto con cambio automatico?

551. I want to leave the car at the airport
Io voglio lasciare l'auto all'aereoporto

552. Where is the tool kit?
Dove è il kit strumenti?

553. We don't need additional insurance!
Non non abbiamo bisogno di un assicurazione aggiuntiva!

554. What is the emergency number?
Quale è il numero di emergenza?

555. Where can I get a taxi?
Dove posso prendere un taxi?

556. Take me to the airport please
Portami all'aereoporto per favore

557. To the bus station please!
Alla stazione dei bus, per favore!

558. Take me to this address
Portami a questo indirizzo

559. Why is it so expensive
Perchè è così costoso

560. I need help with the suitcase
Io ho bisogno di aiuto con il bagaglio

561. Please don't interrupt our conversation
Per favore non interrompere la nostra conversazione

562. Turn off the music!
Abbassa la musica!

Turn down the volume please!
Abbassa il volume per favore

563. Turn on the taximeter
Accendi il tassametro

General Repairs

564. This is damaged
Questo è danneggiato

565. We need tools
Ci servono strumenti

566. Can you repair it?
Puoi ripararlo?

567. Can you do it quickly?
Puoi farlo velocemente?

568. What's the problem?
Quale è il problema?

569. Is it broken?
È rotto?

570. Can you glue it?
Puoi incollarlo?

571. Here is the guarantee
Ecco la garanzia

572. Can you take a look at it?
Puoi darci un occhiata?

573. We need help
Ci serve aiuto

574. We need a specialist
Ci serve uno specialista

575. We need a replacement
Ci serve un ricambio

578. I need nails and a hammer
Io ho bisogno di chiodi e martello

579. I need a saw
Io ho bisogno di una sega

580. Who can fix it?
Chi può sistemarlo?

Church and Religion

581. We are protestants
Noi siamo protestanti

582. We are catholic
Noi siamo cattolici

583. We are muslims
Noi siamo musulmani

584. We are buddhists
Noi siamo buddisti

585. God is above all
Dio è sopra tutto

586. What is your believe?
In cosa credi?

587. My religion is…
La mia religione è...?

588. Do you believe in God?
Credi in Dio?

589. We are a very religious family
Noi siamo una famiglia molto religiosa

590. We go to church on Sundays
Noi andiamo in chiesa la Domenica

591. At what time does the mess start?
A che ora inizia la messa?

592. Where is the synagogue?
Dove è la sinagoga?

593. Where is the mosque?
Dove è la moschea?

594. I would like to see a priest
Io vorrei vedere un prete

596. I would like to pray
Io vorrei pregare

597. Let us pray together
Preghiamo insieme

598. Religious holidays
Feste religliose

599. The bible is important to me
La Bibbia è importante per me

600. Is there a bible study group?
C'è un gruppo di studio della Bibbia qui?

Seasons and Holidays

601. the seasons
Le stagioni

602. spring
primavera

603. summer
estate

604. autumn
autunno

605. winter
inverno

606. January
gennaio

607. february
febbraio

606. March
marzo

607. April
aprile

608. May
maggio

609. June
giugno

610. July
luglio

611. August
agosto

612. September
settembre

613. October
ottobre

614. November
novembre

615. December
dicembre

616. January 1, New Year's Day
1 Gennaio, Capodanno

617. Beginning of holidays
Inizio delle vacanze

618. Main vacation season
Stagione delle vacanze principali

619. Short trip
Breve viaggio

620. Long trips, permanent travelers
Lunghi viaggi, viaggiatori permanenti

621. Holidays / vacation
Vacanze/viaggi

622. Corpus Christi Day
Corpus Domini

623. 15 August, Assumption
15 Agosto, Ferragosto

624. 1. May / International Labor Day
1 Maggio / Festa del lavoro

625. 1 November, All saints Day
1 Novembre, Ognissanti

626. National Holiday
....Name &Date..
**Festa nazionale
…..Nome & Data..**

627. National Family Day
......Name &Date....
**Giorno nazionale della famiglia
….. Nome & Data**

628. 24 December Holy Night
24 Dicembre Vigilia di Natale

629. 25 December, Christmas Day
25 Dicembre, Natale

Flirting and Breaking the Ice with Strangers in Italy

630. Where are you going?
Dove stai andando?

631. Are you here on holidays?
Sei stato qui in vacanza?

632. I would like to invite you
Mi piacerebbe invitarti

633. I doesn't matter
Non mi interessa

634. We are just passing through
Ci siamo appena passati attraverso

635. I can cook for you
Io posso cucinare per te

636. It will be good
Andrà bene

637. Do you know..?
Lo sai..?

638. I can help you
Io posso aiutarti

639. I am good at it
Io lo so fare

640. I need a protection suntan cream
Io ho bisogno di una crema solare

641. What is your favorite color?
Quale è il tuo colore preferito?

642. come / come along!
Vieni / vieni con noi!

643. Can I join you?
Posso unirmi a te?

644. Please wait here
Per favore aspetta qui

645. This is forbidden!
Questo è proibito!

646. Can I smoke here?
Posso fumare qui?

646. Do you have a question?
Hai una domanda?

647. Do you mind if I..?
Intendi se io..?

648. Let's do it together!
Facciamolo insieme!

649. Let's celebrate!
Facciamo festa!

Everyday Words for Travelers

650. open
aperto

651. closed
chiuso

652. hot
caldo

653. cold
freddo

654. beautiful
bello

655. ugly
brutto

656. empty
vuoto

657. full
pieno

658. new
nuovo

659. old
vecchio

660. clean
pulito

661 dirty
sporco

662. bright
luminoso

663. dark
buio

664. cheap
economico

665. expensive
Costoso

666. interesting
interessante

667. boring
noioso

668. friendly
amichevole

669. unfriendly
antipatico

670. nice / pleasant
carino/piacevole

671. a great time
un bel momento

a bad time
un brutto momento

672. lucky
fortunato

bad luck
sfortunato'

673. generous
generoso

674. stingy
avaro

675. honest
onesto

676. dishonest
disonesto

677. free
libero

678. for sale
in vendita

679. to rent
affittasi

680. I agree
Sono d'accordo

Legal Phrases and Terms

681. the deed / title (real estate)
L'intestazione / titolo (mercato immobiliare)

681. the contract
Il contratto

682. real estate contracts are signed by a notary
I contratti immobiliari sono firmati da un notaio

682. to pay a deposit
Pagare un deposito

683. It's already confirmed
è già confermato

684. the witness
Il testimone

685. the judge
Il giudice

686. to denounce
Denunciare

687. criminal charges
Accuse criminali

687. to bail someone
Truffare qualcuno

688. You are accused of...
Sei accusato di...

689. the trial
Il processo

690. I have to go to court
Io devo andare in tribunale

691. lawyer's fee
La parcella dell'avvocato

692. state attorney
Pubblico ministero

693. We need a translator
Ci serve un traduttore

693. Do I have to pay a fine?
Devo pagare una multa?

694. We need a lawyer
Ci serve un avvocato

695. Is it against the law?
Questo è contro la legge?

695. What are the legal requirements?
Quali sono I requisiti legali?

696. We would like to register
Noi vorremmo registrarci

697. What is my legal status?
Quale è il mio stato legale?

698. Who has the custody?
Chi ha la custodia?

699. I am not guilty
Io non sono colpevole

700. I will sue you for fraud
Io ti farò causa per frode

Notes

To improve your Italian reading and your vocabulary we highly recommend getting this book. This bilingual Italian English story book is written for beginners and is suitable for students and teachers alike. Available on all major book platforms.

www.ingramcontent.com/pod-product-compliance
Lightning Source LLC
Chambersburg PA
CBHW042117100526
44587CB00025B/4096